Wonderings

.

Wonderings

Stories of Faith in Life

CARMEN DICELLO

RESOURCE *Publications* · Eugene, Oregon

WONDERINGS
Stories of Faith in Life

Resource Publications
An Imprint of Wipf and Stock Publishers
199 W. 8th Ave., Suite 3
Eugene, OR 97401

www.wipfandstock.com

ISBN 13: 978-1-62032-608-4

Manufactured in the U.S.A.

For those who recognize
That everywhere is hallowed ground
That each day is sacred
And that all of life is God's story

"He taught them by telling many stories."
(Mark 4:2, NLT)

Contents

Acknowledgments

A NUMBER OF PEOPLE played a vital role in the comple-
tion of this manuscript. Many thanks to Dr. Rick Walston,
who proofread most of it and offered valuable suggestions
along the way. Jason Crowder provided a number of helpful ideas, including the suggestion for the title, Wonderings. My brother, Mark "Moke" DiCello, who sacrificed a
good amount of time and energy perusing the manuscript,
encouraged me to pursue publication. Bruno Tassone
has for years been a wise conversation partner (KP!). My
students at Pottsville Area High School are a consistent
source of inspiration.

Also, I would like to thank Steve Gunderson, Rick
Kantner, and Rick Wade, along with Jason Crowder men-
tioned above, for their willingness to endorse this project.
Your support and kind words are very much appreciated.

I am grateful for the diligent efforts of those whose
help and expertise made it possible for these essays to be
brought to print. Natalie Turner of FreelancePermissions.
com acquired permissions. The good people at Wipf &
Stock, especially Christian Amondson, worked patiently
with me throughout the publication process.

Above all, I am so thankful for my fantastic wife,
Marilyn, and my wonderful boys, Luke and Jake. As we
journey together, God's presence in our lives becomes

Acknowledgments

increasingly clear, as does the reality of how incredibly blessed I am. I love you guys!.

Introduction

IT HAS BEEN SAID that God speaks to us in all of life. In the physical universe, through our relationships and circumstances, and in various other ways, the Maker of all things makes himself known.[1] In a very real sense, therefore, our lives are the amphitheater upon which the Lord of heaven and earth plays his songs of wonder and love.

One of the ways that God manifests himself most profoundly is through stories. The Christian Scriptures are, to a large extent, a compilation of stories that in various ways speak to the issue of the relationship we can and should have with our Creator.

The greatest story of them all, of course, is the story of Jesus. And one of the primary avenues by which he conveyed spiritual realities was through teaching, specifically teaching by means of metaphor and parable.

Jesus saw in the world around him a variety of ways to depict greater truths about God, human beings, and other matters of immense significance. In similar (though

---

1. The most clear of God's revelations is his Son, Jesus, who is the revelation of God par excellence. He, along with the Scriptures that point to him, is sometimes referred to as special revelation. Still, the God who speaks to us in "special" ways is the same God who personalizes his relationship with us through the various facets of our lives.

obviously less authoritative) ways, we too are able to utilize stories to express truths that provide wisdom and facilitate our link with God. In some profound and liberating way, God meets us in stories.

The following personal reflections highlight essential spiritual priorities, emphasizing truths that inform, encourage, and enliven. My hope is that these *Wonderings* will resonate within you, inspiring a keen awareness of the story God is telling in and through your life and stirring you to follow him each day.

PART 1

Faith's Meaning

Any truly meaningful faith must be an informed faith.
Genuine belief must be distinguished
from weak or counterfeit alternatives.
Faith thrives when it is properly grasped.

1

Cross the Bridge

the meaning of believe

IT'S A COMMON PIECE of advice. "Trust the Lord." "You've got to believe." "Keep the faith." But how are we to understand faith? What is it that we are supposed to keep?

In its most basic sense, faith involves believing in something or someone. Men and women, young and old, rich and poor—we are all called to faith. And this faith is a personal thing, entailing belief in the only rightful object of faith, the living God. This God, according to Christian teaching, created human beings to know him. But we have abandoned our created purpose, which is why this same God has intervened in human affairs, seeking to rescue us from ourselves and so reestablish a relationship with us. This he did most profoundly through his unique emissary and Son, Jesus. At its core, faith looks to him. Still, not all people believe, and even those who do believe often demonstrate varying degrees of faith. Perhaps an illustration will help to clarify.

Each year, my family travels from our home in Pennsylvania to Cape May, New Jersey, our usual vacation destination. On the way to Cape May, we travel through Philadelphia and across the Walt Whitman Bridge. It is of course possible to know about the Walt Whitman without having seen it. You can read about it or acquire knowledge of it from someone familiar with the bridge. Assuming reliable resources, you would be fairly confident about the existence of the bridge and certain facts about it. Then, if someone were to ask you about the bridge, you would be able to provide a measure of useful information. This knowledge constitutes a type of faith. In other words you would have faith that there is a bridge called Walt Whitman.

Then again, it is also possible to travel to Philadelphia in order to catch a glimpse of the bridge for yourself. You might park your car near the bridge and observe its sturdiness and how well it supports the many automobiles that traverse it each day. Not only would you then know about the bridge, having heard of it from others, but you'd be convinced that it is durable and provides a safe connection between Pennsylvania and New Jersey. After all, you would have seen how well it worked for others. Again, your knowledge of the bridge and its capabilities is a kind of faith.

But all that you've done so far is only preliminary to the much more personal use of the Walt Whitman Bridge. If you really want to make use of the bridge, you have to cross it yourself. This involves more than facts (that there is a bridge called Walt Whitman) and even more than acceptance of those facts (that the Walt Whitman is safe and travel-worthy). It requires trust, actual personal commitment to the Walt Whitman Bridge. In other words you must actually travel across the bridge, relying on its ability to sustain you and lead you to your destination.

True faith is a lot like this. While it surely benefits from research and is inspired by the faith of others, it also goes to the next level, resting in faith's object, depending on God's promises, and trusting in God's reliability.

Faith, then, is trust in the truth of God and in the God of truth. To believe is to cast your hopes, day by day and sometimes moment by moment, upon the One who has pledged his love to you. Given that we are the ones who must believe, and recognizing how fickle and foolish we can be, it is not at all surprising that faith tends to fluctuate. But the issue is not how much faith we have, for Jesus mentioned that faith the size of a mustard seed could move a mountain (Matthew 17:20). And it's not how impressive our faith appears to others, for this can lead to hypocrisy (Matthew 6:1; 23:5). What truly matters is that our faith is in the One who does not fluctuate, who promises to journey with us through this world, and who is "the same yesterday and today and forever" (Hebrews 13:8).

When it comes to the Walt Whitman, we can learn about the bridge and observe others who travel across it. Similarly, it is helpful to gain information about our Creator, observing others who look to him. But, ultimately, we ourselves must trust in him. That's what genuine is faith is all about, and that's what we are all called to do. Cross the bridge and believe.

2

Invisible Yet Real
connecting to the living God

ONE OF MY FONDEST memories is of my seminary experience. After years of attempting to further my education through traditional means, the time and distance involved in these efforts were beginning to wear me out. It seemed like it would take many years and much hassle to complete a degree program.

Therefore, it was a major revelation to discover that there were non-traditional ways of earning a degree. Specifically, I learned of a long distance educational program through a school named Columbia Evangelical Seminary (CES). CES operates in much the same way as the British educational model. Basically, you work with an adviser/ scholar, and together you construct a program of studies.[1]

1. For more information see http://www.columbiaseminary.org.

Part 1: Faith's Meaning

My adviser through my Master of Divinity and Doctor of Theological Studies programs was Dr. Rick Walston, the president of the seminary. I first spoke with Dr. Walston over the phone, and I immediately sensed a connection between the two of us. Thus, when he offered to be my academic guide, I quickly accepted.

Over the course of time, Rick and I worked together in structuring my programs. He gave me suggestions, pointed out weaknesses in my methodology, challenged my presuppositions, and helped shape me into a more effective thinker and writer.

As the years went by, Rick and I had many conversations. As a result, we got to know one another better. This, in turn, led to a number of non-school-related projects. Sometimes, he would ask me to proofread a paper he had written. Or, I would ask the same of him. On other occasions, we swapped personal stories or laughed together about things that struck us as particularly humorous. Over time, we interacted about a host of subjects, and for a variety of reasons.

As we got to know one another, a friendship ensued. In fact I would consider Rick one of my closest friends and advisors. He's someone I can count on, whose words I highly respect, and a person with whom I often seem to be "on the same page." I look forward to many years of continuing camaraderie.

Having offered this synopsis, I think it is important to point out one very important fact: Rick and I have never actually met![2] All of our discussions have taken place via the internet and through telephone conversations. Though he is my spiritual and intellectual friend, I have never shaken

---

2. Since I originally penned this chapter, I have indeed seen Rick face-to-face. We got together for a short time during a trip he made to the east coast. At least temporarily, we spent some time together.

his hand, stared him in the eye, or visited his home. Though he is my friend, I have never actually seen him.

I tell this story not only to share a bit of my personal history, but to illustrate a point, which is this: It is possible and reasonable to sustain a relationship with someone whom you cannot see. That is, you can get to know and appreciate a person you have not yet officially "met."

In light of this illustration, it is fascinating to consider the claims often made by skeptics about the existence and nature of God. Some ask, "How can I believe in someone whom I am not able to see?" Others say, "If God were real, I'd be able to identify him more clearly." Or, "Your God is merely a figment of your imagination, a hopeful creation of the human mind."

For those who think these and similar thoughts, I recount my relationship with Rick Walston, for in some ways it mirrors the relationship people can have with God. For instance Rick is, in one sense, very far removed from me; he lives in Washington State, while I reside in Pennsylvania. In another sense, however, Rick is very near to me, a phone call or an email away. God is like that, too. He is, after all, an invisible being. Yet, at the same time, he is near to all who call on his name.

Likewise, I have seen pictures of Rick. Some of them show him being serious and others jovial. But in all of them, I catch a glimpse of what Rick is like. Similarly, God has given us "pictures" of himself. We see these "pictures" in nature, in his followers, and, of course, most profoundly, in his written Word and in his Son, Jesus. As Jesus said, "He who has seen Me has seen the Father" (John 14:9).

Consider also that Rick and I have often spoken of getting together at some point, traveling to one another's homes. We've discussed the times we'll share, hanging out together, eating pizza, and simply talking through the night.

Part 1: Faith's Meaning

It is a real hope of ours that we will one day get together. Again, this resembles Scripture's portrayal of a relationship with God. While we know him truly, and though our relationship with him deepens, we look forward to the day when we will be able to see him face-to-face.

Of course no analogy is perfect, including this one. Indeed, every illustration or parable breaks down at some point. When it comes to God, all an analogy can hope to do is express some aspect or facet of that which defies full explanation. This being said, the analogy given here will hopefully provide at least a glimpse into what the divine-human connection is like.

If you are a believer, take heart when you are questioned about your belief in an invisible God. Though you have not seen him, his presence in this world is undeniably real and powerful. Likewise, you can look forward to the time when faith gives way to sight, when full disclosure takes place.

Then again, you may be one of those skeptics mentioned earlier. If this is the case, I would ask you to consider that life is often more complex and wonderful than you've imagined. It is true that many of God's ways are hidden from our view. But what should we expect? After all, he is a spirit being, a non-corpuscular entity, a transcendent Lord. Scripture's depiction of God fits what we find in our daily experiences of him.

But this is not the entire story, for the elusive God is also with us. Indeed, he took on our nature in the person of his Son. Through Jesus, we have free access to our Maker. Countless individuals, including some former skeptics, have experienced his grace, love, and mysterious presence.

Perhaps, you are still not convinced. If so, why don't you ask God to reveal himself to you? Prayerfully consider his ways. Look for him in Scripture and everywhere in your life. Remain open to his disclosures. Today, call on him.

The true God is a God of surprises, a deity whose ways often go against human expectations. One of these "surprises" involves the amazing relationship we can have with our invisible Creator. Though imperceptible to the human eye, God's ways are detectable to those who are willing to see, for he has left an indelible impression in many places and on innumerable hearts. Many of us already know this to be the case, for he has "emailed" and "telephoned" us on many occasions. Have you checked your messages lately?

3

No Sweat!

what to do when we are the problem

SOME TIME AGO, A bunch of us got together to play a little basketball. The gym where we gathered was particularly hot that day, and the air was thick. What made matters worse for me, though, is the fact that I perspire more than normal human beings. To put it plainly, I tend to sweat like a pig. I mean, it is typical for me to change my shirt three, four, or even five times during an hour-and-a-half bout of exercise. I sweat a lot.

At any rate, as we were playing basketball, it became clear to me that the court was getting quite slick. By the time we took our first break, many drops of perspiration spotted the floor, making for a potentially treacherous surface. Recognizing the slippery conditions, I reached into my gym bag, grabbed a towel, and began to walk around the court, wiping up sweat wherever it appeared.

Part 1: Faith's Meaning

As I made my way across the floor, I noticed that one of the other players was getting a kick out of what I was doing. Initially, it was unclear what he found so amusing. Then, fighting back the laughter, he revealed the humor of the situation. "Hey," he said, "you're only making things worse!" As I perceived what I was doing, it quickly dawned on me what he meant. You see, even as I was trying to wipe away the drops of perspiration that had fallen to the ground, I was simultaneously leaving watery puddles wherever I walked. By the time I traveled the length of the court, I had left a trail of even more perspiration. As my friend noted, I was not helping things at all.

The moral of the story is easy enough: A sweating man should not be put in charge of wiping up a slippery surface. Or, to generalize a bit more, sometimes our efforts to make things better actually make them much worse.

Although this basketball debacle probably has numerous applications, it initially reminded me of the way many of us act when it comes to spiritual matters. If someone were to ask you how you can know God, properly relating to him, how would you answer? Many people think God will accept them if they built a pretty good reputation. According to this way of thinking, good deeds, religious devotion, and similar commitments assure one that all is well between themselves and God.

There is of course nothing wrong with good deeds, religious devotion, and the like. In fact there is much that is right about a properly nuanced approach to such practices. The problem with these and similar sentiments, however, is that those who sincerely believe they can impress God with their spiritual résumés fail to recognize that even as they seek to eliminate bad habits and cultivate good ones, they are still, to use our analogy, sweating profusely. Amid their moral and religious pursuits, they have neglected to see that everything they do is tainted with human imperfection.

If good works is the path you've chosen for earning heaven's favor, make sure you are conscious of how far short you fall of you own standards, let alone God's. Whenever you attempt to clean up the messes of your past, don't forget that you continue to create new messes in your efforts along the way. No matter your earnestness or skill at dabbing up the beads of "sweat" you've deposited, your efforts are quite ineffective. If it weren't so serious, we too might laugh at the results.

All people intuitively know that goodness matters, and that God wants us to be like him. The mistake we make, however, is in overestimating our own ability to achieve genuine goodness, to wipe up the "perspiration" we leave wherever we go. Likewise, through neglect or ignorance, we fail to look for someone who can truly rescue us from the chaos of our past, present, and future.

What, then, is the solution to this dilemma? What does a "sweating" person do when faced with the realization that sweating is a way of life, when misbehavior and despicable tendencies are the hallmarks of our daily existence? Our own towels won't work. That much is clear. What we need is someone who doesn't sweat. What we require, in other words, is a perfect person, who can wipe up the mess that we've made. And who can do that? Jesus can.

What about you? Are you leaving a trail of sweat? Is your world becoming increasingly unsafe because of the choices you've made? Have you come to the conclusion that the more effort you make at cleaning up your life, the more precarious it becomes. If so, it's time to put down your towel and to stop pretending that you can impress God or change your life through sheer self-effort. It's time to allow the only "sweat-free" person, the faultless Jesus, to clean away the mess that you've made.

> Yet we know that a person is made right with God by faith in Jesus Christ, not by obeying the law. And we have believed in Christ Jesus, so that we might be made right with God because of our faith in Christ, not because we have obeyed the law. For no one will ever be made right with God by obeying the law (Galatians 2:16, NLT)

If you feel so inclined, you can go to him right now. By his stand-in-your-place death and his death-defeating emergence from the grave, he accomplished all that is required to make you right before God. Yes, he can and will wipe away the perspiration from your life. For him, it's no sweat!

4

Not as Close as You Might Think

sobering thoughts on religious options

IT WAS PLAIN TO see:

| Hazleton 67 |
| Allentown 66 |

That's what the road sign read, as we made the return trip along Route 81 from Harrisburg to Pottsville.

What struck me about the sign was what it seemed to imply. Clearly, or so it appeared, Allentown and Hazleton are located just one mile apart. This being the case, the short distance between these two cities might be traversed in very little time. Likewise, cities this close might have a lot in common, and the residents of either city would, no doubt, be familiar with one another.

There's just one problem with this interpretation, which is this: Allentown and Hazleton are actually not as close as you might think. In fact, as a quick look at a map reveals, they are actually eighty miles apart! You see, the sign that listed these distances is located on a highway that eventually splits. Some seven miles or so down the road from where we first saw the sign, one must choose between two routes, one south, toward Allentown, and the other north, toward Hazleton. The situation looks like this:

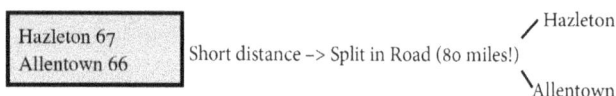

Hazleton 67
Allentown 66   Short distance –> Split in Road (80 miles!)

Hazleton
Allentown

Somehow, all of this reminds me of the spiritual landscape of our day and the way many people talk about religion. For certain religious pluralists, the idea that all roads lead to God is axiomatic. Indeed, it is assumed that the many spiritual options are but expressions of the same reality, and that all efforts to embody the sacred are pretty much alike. They are like cities, separated by a short distance.

Of course there are some relative similarities between the many systems of religion. Just like Allentown and Hazleton, so religions have a relative proximity to one another. Most of them point to a Supreme Being, many promote a sense of morality and accountability, and all of them are an acknowledgment, however imperfect, of the human longing for the transcendent. All of this is good and even expected, for it would be strange if God failed to manifest himself through those who bear his image. Given that the various adherents and advocates of religion are creatures who reflect their Creator, it makes sense to find some measure of spiritual activity and agreement amid the religions.

This said, it is also important to point out that the similarities between the numerous religious options must not distract us from noticing the differences. To this end, the bold claims of Jesus come to mind. After all, he declared that we cannot enter into a relationship with our Maker apart from him (John 14:6). Furthermore, only Jesus, among the religious contenders, claimed to be God incarnate, offered his life as a ransom for human beings, absorbed the penalty due human impropriety, and eventually defeated the grave. What's more, Jesus alone offers to draw near to us in a unique relationship that combines Lordship (i.e., he's in charge) with friendship (i.e., he's our closest confidant). Whether you accept or reject these claims, it is hard to deny that they are quite unlike any other system of belief.

What we discover, therefore, is that—just as we observed with the road sign—some religious alternatives are not as close to one another as certain pundits propound. Though it is common to place all faith convictions within the same rubric, in reality there is a split in the road, and the way of Jesus does not coincide with or completely parallel the other options.

It is at this juncture that we must face the proverbial fork in the road, for the choices we make can determine the direction of our lives and our ultimate destinies. Numerous views vie for our attention, and some of them may appear not much different than the message of Jesus. But, as the fork makes clear, they can actually be many miles apart. There are numerous philosophies that are based on the effort to impress God with morality and/or religious observance. In contrast the way of Jesus offers eternal life for free, a direct link to God through his Son, and spiritual liberty through access to the living God.

Let's be honest, though, certain religious options *do* bring a measure of fulfillment, many of them will lead to a close relationship with your fellow man, and some of them might possibly be steps along the way to a connection with God. However, and this is the point, only Jesus can lead you, how shall we put it, all the way to God, enabling you to experience true and abundant life.

What about you? Have you considered not only the similarities between the world's religious options but the differences? Don't allow the similarities to blind you to the dissimilarities. Don't allow partial truths to hinder you from embracing the One who is the truth. Don't let your present location on the road of life deceive you into thinking that all spiritual offerings and leaders are pretty much alike. When the road splits, the differences will become obvious. After all, Allentown and Hazleton, like life and death, like heaven and hell, like truth and error, aren't as close as you might think.

5

Just Believe?

locating faith's object

JUST BELIEVE. YOU HEAR it all the time. It's become something of mantra: "Believe. Believe! Believe!!" So prevalent is this approach to life that even Weight Watchers[1] has taken to promoting the idea that believing is the key to weight loss.

In one sense, of course, there is a great truth to the—what shall we call it?—believing philosophy. If by *belief* we mean simply "believe in who you are," this can indeed be an impetus, an incentive, to positive change. Self-confidence often produces a strong determination to accomplish whatever it is that we set our minds to do. Furthermore, it is surely the case that for many the "believe" mindset is shorthand for "trust in that which transcends you." Look to God, in other words. This, too, is a good thing.

1. See http://www.weightwatchers.com.

Part 1: Faith's Meaning

On the other hand, there is also a tendency, I think, to assume that the sheer act of believing is enough, and that heaven somehow smiles on whatever acts of sincerity and faith we can muster. While sincerity is indeed a non-negotiable aspect of any worthy endeavor, it is surely the case that sincere faith in whatever strikes one's fancy, even if faith's object is unworthy, or faith in one's own power to believe, is simply inadequate.

Let's say, for instance, that we believe the moon is made of green cheese. Though we might sincerely believe this to be the case, we will surely be disappointed if we actually travel to the moon in search of a little slice of it. Or, to provide another example, we might sincerely believe a certain pill will improve our physical wellbeing. But if that pill turns out to be cyanide, it not only won't help but will prove harmful. No matter how strong our "faith," it is mistaken (and potentially dangerous) if it is misplaced.

Faith, to be clear, entails trust in something or in someone. We trust in a reliable friend. We trust a faithful spouse. We trust the stability of the bridge we are traversing.[2] Faith is acting on truth, relying on something or someone.

But if this is indeed what we mean by faith, it is quite evident that it is only as good as the thing or person in which we believe. To trust in an individual with questionable character is to prepare for disappointment. Reliance on someone with unimpeachable character, on the other hand, is likely to produce better results.

So it is when it comes to spiritual matters. There are numerous illustrations of people who trust in themselves, false or imaginary deities, or their own religious résumés. But as many have pointed out, some of these options are bogus, and it's not because God has set up some arbitrary criteria for delineating right from wrong. No, the reason is

2. See Chapter 1, Cross the Bridge.

because they are spiritual counterfeits. The reason is that they do not ultimately produce what they promise. The reason is because God wants us all to recognize that he alone is our ultimate source of help and sustenance. The reason is that they run contrary to the very being of God. The essence of authentic worship is finding in God our created purpose, locating hope and joy in the One who made us. Placing our faith anywhere else or in anyone else is misplaced. Faith must seek its proper object. Believe, yes, but believe specifically in that which is worthy of faith.

It is here that we often enter into controversy. In a pluralistic world, all options are supposed to be equally valid. Indeed, to suggest otherwise is considered by many a kind of social blasphemy.

Well, sorry to disappoint the secular pundits, but the "all views are equally valid" perspective is simply self-refuting.

Think about it. If you claim that all views are valid, and I say they are not, how are we to make sense of your assertion? If what you say is true, then my view must also be true. But for my view to be true, yours would have to be false.

If, on the other hand, you deny or suppress my view—in essence declaring that my opinion is invalid—then you are contradicting your own original supposition (i.e., that all views are valid).

Of course at this point some might back off slightly, claiming the "all views are valid" idea is hyperbolic. Thus, proponents might argue, while not all views are legitimate, at least many of them are. In some things this is indeed the case. If we were to have an apple pie-making contest, it is likely that, personal favorites aside, numerous pies would be adequate. However, if we were discussing the best angle for reentry of a craft from outer space, the options would become severely limited. At that point, every opinion would not be acceptable, or necessarily safe.

Part 1: Faith's Meaning

To place this within the religious sphere, it is again self-evident that all views cannot possibly be saying the same thing, certainly not when they make major claims that contradict the claims of other religious alternatives.

So, how then do we decide which view is best? Well, we might examine the available evidence, compare what we find with personal observation, ask whether what we are being told to believe actually fits the world in which we live, etc. Here, however, we won't delve into these and other areas, for the immediate points are simply that it is ludicrous to assert that all views are equally valid, and it is likewise perfectly reasonable to assert that there is a proper object of faith.

To this end, the Christian worldview affirms that there is a true God, who has revealed himself in abundant ways but most clearly and meaningfully in his Son, Jesus. He is the object of faith par excellence. The Jesus perspective, if we can call it that, is a long and honorable tradition that is abundantly supported by much evidence, corresponds to what we find in the real world, and has sustained, enlivened, and transformed billions of people. Furthermore, it both assumes and asserts that not all views are correct, thus making a distinction between truth and error.

Of course none of this automatically establishes anything about genuine faith. Nor does it eliminate every controversy or necessarily reduce the ire of those who—for good or bad reasons—refuse to remain open to faith. It does, however, provide clarity for those who desire it and hope for those who, while recognizing that not all ways lead to God, grasp the notion that Jesus did indeed assert—because it is true and truth is what's best for us—that he can and does lead his followers all the way to God.

What about those who never hear? What about those unable to grasp the simple truths of the faith? What about those whose understanding is severally hampered by ignorance or misunderstanding? The questions remain, and often they baffle.

But the central tenet of faith remains the same, and it makes a whole lot more sense than the pluralistic assertions of those who want to treat all views as essentially equal. All claims cannot be true. And only one has the combined benefits of being historical, humanely relevant, theistic, realistic, victorious, hopeful, accessible, and free.[3]

Amid countless claims, including many naïve and self-defeating assertions, Jesus words continue to reverberate across the corridors of time and resonate within the human spirit: "*I* am the way."

---

3. To expand on each of these, the Christian faith is historical because what Jesus accomplished was not a theory but revolved around historical occurrences. It is both humanely relevant, for Jesus was indeed a man, and theistic, for Jesus claimed to be God's unique emissary and Son. Likewise, it is realistic because it honestly confronts the realities of human frailty and impropriety. The faith is also victorious, with the claim that Jesus overcame the grave, and hopeful, in that men and women are given both temporal and eternal hope in the living Savior. Furthermore, God is truly accessible, for all are invited to participate, and it is free, since a right standing with God is the result not of human performance but of trusting in Jesus' performance.

6

Typing and Knowing

intuition and faith

A SHORT TIME AGO, I sat down at a computer in the school where I teach. As is typical, I had to type in my password in order to access my school account. So, that's what I did; I began to type my password—something I have done many times—but for some reason I couldn't log on. I typed slowly and carefully, and I even questioned whether I had confused my password with something else.

But the more I pondered my situation, the more it didn't make sense. I *knew* I had the correct password, and I was certainly pressing the correct corresponding keys. Or, was I? As I tried and retried my password, something didn't feel right. It seemed like something was a little out of kilter.

At that point, I decided to abandon the slow and meticulous strategy and take an instinctual approach. That is, I would type my password as I normally do, very quickly and without a lot of thought. As I did this, I discovered something quite surprising. The keys on the computer key-board had been switched! Someone had decided to play a trick on whoever would use this computer next, switching two of the keys. I believe it was a "C" for a "V."

Though this kind of thing doesn't happen all of the time, it is not completely surprising given that I teach in a high school; kids can be mischievous. What *was* surprising, however, is the manner in which I discovered this change. You see, I don't technically know where the keys are. Though I have been typing for many years, I've never had any formal instruction. If someone were to ask me to correctly label a typing template, I'm pretty sure I'd fail. However, this does not mean that I am unable to type. Indeed, the opposite is true, and through many years of practice I have become quite proficient and relatively quick. I "know" the keys instinctively.

The intriguing thing is that while I did not know exactly where the keys should have been located, I *did* have a sense of "knowing" where the keys ought to have been. Knowledge, in other words, is not limited to the rote memory variety. There is a different type of knowing that occurs, often through practice, the kind of gut-instinct knowledge of which we are all familiar.

This instinctive knowledge can be explained in a number of ways. Some simply label it a gut feeling or intuition. Others, utilizing theological jargon, relate it to the *sensus divinitatis*, an awareness of higher things placed there by God. But whatever the precise terminology, there seems to be in all of us an awareness of some larger purpose, a hunch, suspicion, or instinct that we are not alone. This hunch, Christian thinkers would argue, is grounded in our connectedness to God. There is something in us that corresponds to something in God.

When I sat down at the computer, I wasn't aware of the key-switch. But the solution, in this case, was not found through in-depth research and the like. Rather, I solved this problem when I followed my intuition and allowed my hands to instinctively locate the right keys. So it can be with God. There are times when we have to extend ourselves beyond that which we can observe, embracing the simple but profound reality that we are wired for God. When we recognize this instinct and respond in faith, the One who is faith's object often becomes that much clearer to us.[1]

Of course it is entirely proper to look for evidence of God's presence, to personally research what we are able in our quest for increased meaning, in our search for God. In other words we can surely access God through investigation and analysis of his world and ways. But beyond and supplementing our own discoveries is the ongoing truth that God is present, and we are built to know him. Just like there was something almost innate about my awareness of computer keys, so we all possess a sense of the divine. Mystifying as it may be, it is nonetheless real.

So, as you pursue things spiritual and explore various interests, don't neglect the intuitive facet of faith. If God has indeed made us for himself, if we are created in his image, there is likely an otherworldly (or was that this-worldly?) echo that we can pick up if we allow ourselves to remain open to the ever-present God. Sometimes, you can study "the keys" and learn about this or that feature of reality. Other times, whatever the "keys" may appear to say, it's best to follow your inner inklings, your suspicions, and your sense of what seems to be inescapably true. Every

---

1. This parallels what Jesus says in John 7:17 "If anyone is willing to do His will, he will know of the teaching, whether it is of God or whether I speak from Myself." In other words when we align ourselves with God's purpose—which is an act of faith—this alignment somehow connects us to God and provides access to truths that are otherwise unavailable.

now and then, you just know that certain things are right, that you were created *by* God and *for* God.[2]

2. None of this "instinctive language" is intended to deny that human beings are also born corrupt (see Romans 3:23). In the words of Scripture, "a natural man does not accept the things of the Spirit of God, for they are foolishness to him; and he cannot understand them, because they are spiritually appraised" (1 Corinthians 2:14). Human apathy and antipathy toward the things of God must be lifted and overcome if any of us are to follow our "instincts" all the way to God. Ultimately, however, this is God's business and his prerogative. Our duty, primarily, is to simply invite people to embrace the ever-present God.

7

Metanoia

the ongoing need to change

"Repent!" I have to admit that I don't particularly like the term. Often, it comes across as an arbitrary emotional appeal designed to by-pass common-sense and the intellect, an effort to produce a feeling of guilt, a manipulative ploy in which people are harangued into jumping through various religious hoops. A certain (earned) reputation often accompanies those who use such language. I can't help but recall the countless times when I've been embarrassed by the idiosyncrasies of those who incessantly cried, "Repent!"

But, lest we allow our antipathy to fundamentalist caricatures to hinder our progress in (or toward) faith, it is important to proceed with balance. Though "repent" may leave a bad taste in your mouth, the actual meaning of the concept is quite sensible and spiritually germane.

The Greek term for repent is *metanoia*, and it represents an idea that it quite prevalent in the New Testament. Basically, *metanoia* means "to turn." It is used in a variety of contexts and implies both a "turning from" that which is harmful and spiritually damaging and a "turning to" that which is good and spiritually rejuvenating. When put this way, the notion of repentance sounds relevant, for we all need to be reminded to stay away from whatever endangers us and to stay near whatever is beneficial. This is what we tell our children, is it not? Likewise, we use such words when we're trying to assist family members or friends who need to make wise choices. Repentance, then—the idea if not always the actual term—is something we are all aware of.

If we were to describe *metanoia*, it would include: turning from selfishness to selflessness, from arrogance to humility, from personal autonomy ("I can pretty much get along on my own") to reliance on others and God, from pompous close-mindedness to sensible openness, from inappropriate behaviors to helpful and honorable ones, from dishonesty to integrity, from going your own way to following Jesus into the unknown. It would be easy to multiply the examples.

Of course to provide these samples is to uncover our own inconsistencies, our fickle tendencies. Therefore, or so it would seem, the *metanoia* spoken of here is not simply a once and done deal but rather an attitude that, once begun, continues throughout one's lifetime. And if that is the case, we are faced with the issue of what we are accountable to, or to whom, and this brings us squarely to Jesus and to his call.

Early in his ministry, Jesus put it this way: "Follow Me." He said it in a number of different settings and to a variety of people, but the basic message remained the same: "Follow Me." At the end of the day *metanoia* is about acknowledging that he is worth following. It's not about strange religious garb or weird personal habits. It's not about living in a bubble, separated from reality. It's not about some sort of monastic existence or abandoning one's personality and gifts. Rather, it's about allowing this carpenter's son to shape and give purpose to your personality and provide direction in the use of your gifts. Indeed, it's about recognizing that your gifts actually originate in him.

What this means, of course, is that *metanoia* may not be such a bad idea after all. Indeed, it might be our highest calling, for it challenges us daily to walk with purpose and integrity, motivated and empowered by the One who governs our lives and gives us hope.

How, then, should we respond? That's simple: Repent . . . or, if you prefer, turn . . . or, better yet, run away from everything that is foolish and harmful, and wholeheartedly pursue all that is proper and noble. When put this way, *metanoia* sounds like a pretty good thing.

8

If Necessary, Use Words

what faith does

> "Preach the gospel at all times.
> If necessary, use words."
>
> —SAINT FRANCIS OF ASSISI

ONE OF MY GOOD friends, and among the most impressive individuals I know, is a man by the name of Rick. Though Rick fairly recently became a pastor, he has been a train engineer for many years.

When working on the railroad, Rick obviously has a variety of duties to perform. But, as in any field, he also mingles with co-workers, and along the way he is able to have an impact in their lives.

Part 1: Faith's Meaning

Another friend, Tom, is also a train engineer, who worked alongside of Rick and got to know him. In the early days, Rick was a believer, but Tom was not. However, as the two of them spent time together, Tom sensed something different about Rick, something spiritual that Tom was missing.

Eventually, Tom became a believer, and Rick explained many of the important issues of theology. But the truly amazing thing about their relationship is that it took Rick well over four years before he mentioned anything explicit about the Christian faith.

Contrary to the opinion of some, Rick's "silence" was not at all a failure on his part to meet certain evangelistic requirements. Though he had worked with Tom on many occasions, Rick never felt compelled to force-feed the truth to Tom. Rick wasn't concerned about bombarding Tom with a myriad of facts about the faith. Instead, he simply lived in front of Tom, discussing daily affairs, and doing whatever it is that train engineers do.

You see, Rick had not neglected the gospel. Indeed, he had preached it everyday. This, in fact, explained Tom's interest in spiritual things, and it also became the human factor in Tom's ultimate conversion. Though Rick was more than happy to verbally clarify the faith, his first and most pertinent responsibility was that of living out his faith before Tom.[1]

Rick's positive behavior provides a perfect example of spiritual priorities, which is what Saint Francis sought to

1. The point, of course, is not that we must wait for some lengthy period of time to elapse before opening our mouths, and certainly there are occasions when it is completely appropriate to speak the truth early in our relationships with others. There is no timetable when it comes to verbally sharing the gospel. The primary point is that our lives must match the message we believe. Indeed, it is often the case that we have ample opportunity to preach with our lives before we do so with our words.

highlight in the above quote. While it obviously matters what we say with our mouths, and though truth must be spoken, even more relevant is the way we conduct ourselves each day.

It is amazing how often we get this backwards, treating our formulations and treatises as if they are the end-all of anything spiritual. Of course words are relevant. Jesus spoke words; indeed, he is the Word. Scripture itself involves words, words that lead to life. Clearly, we cannot operate for very long without invoking language and seeking to apply it to our lives. However, and this is the point, words *alone* are never enough. Indeed, even the words we rightly embrace are words intended, in the final analysis, to transform us.

What Saint Francis is saying is that God is not so much concerned about a series of well-crafted theological formulas or a proper articulation of the good news. These obviously matter; that much is clear. But the purpose of the truth we have acquired, the intent of the gospel, is to actually find its way into our hearts and lives, dramatically altering the way we live, love, and relate to others.

When we are in heaven, the core of our existence will involve *being*—being what we were created to be, being for one another what we only imperfectly fulfilled while here, being image-bearers of divine love and truth.[2]

---

2. When we are in heaven, we will fulfill what God intended for us all along. We will "be" all that he designed us to be (1 John 3:2). In this setting we will certainly communicate, which will no doubt involve the use of words. As glorified human beings, we will behave, think, speak, and relate to others in ways that honor God and achieve his purpose. Given that this is the goal of our union with God, this "being" (and all that it entails) is to commence even now (Hebrews 12:1–2). In the context of this chapter, we are to be both speaking and, as St. Francis reminds us, embodying the truth.

So it is now. Words are significant, very significant, but nothing compares to a changed life, and few things alter the outlook of others more than a life that "preaches" all day long.

Our lives ought to exude compassion and kindness. The good news—the news that we are loved and accepted, that we are empowered to love, that we have purpose—should flow from our lives in such a way that no one can deny it. Now, being realistic, we can anticipate many a blunder and countless inconsistencies, at least I know I can. But, to the extent that we accept this challenge, this mission, we will be most effective when we pay attention to the priorities of Jesus: "Let your light shine before men in such a way that they see your good works, and glorify your Father who is in heaven" (Matthew 5:16). Here's another one: "By this all men will know you are my disciples, if you have love for one another" (John 13:35). Or, in the words of Paul: "Whatever you do in word or deed, do all in the name of the Lord Jesus" (Colossians 3:17)—words plus deeds: there's the balance.

As Tom can testify, he witnessed the truth long before he understood it intellectually. Such was the influence of Rick, who is a wonderful model of what Saint Francis is trying to convey. Preach the gospel at all times. Wherever you are and whatever you are doing, preach the gospel. Be it morning, afternoon, or evening, preach the gospel. Whether it's raining or the sun is shining, let the good news, the message of faith, hope, and love, emanate from your life. And, when it's needed, when the situation and setting warrant it, open your mouth too. Preach the gospel at all times. If necessary, use words.

PART 2

Faith's Hurdles

Believers are not removed from the perils of daily existence
but fortified amid hazardous situations.
As faith responds to life's challenges, it flourishes.

9

Doubt

learning to see in the dark

LET'S FACE IT. THERE have been times when you've wondered about it all. Perhaps, you've questioned the goodness
of God, whether he cares about you. Maybe, you've gone
through times of uncertainty, unclear as to whether this
"faith thing" actually works. Or, perhaps, the thought has
crossed your mind that theism itself, the belief that there
is a God, might be wrong. What if it's all a bunch of bunk?

A number of years ago, I struggled with issues relating to the identity of Jesus. I would go for a jog that often
took me past a local synagogue, and I would ask myself if
Jesus, far from being the Son of God, was merely a first cen-
tury Jew who made a big splash in his day.[1] I recall being

---

1. In what might be considered a piece of historical irony, this same
synagogue was purchased by a Christian church. Thus, the building
that once caused me to wonder if Jesus was simply a man is now oc-
cupied by a group that acknowledges his deity.

plagued with doubt about the resurrection. It wasn't that I had studied the facts and found them unreasonable. Quite the opposite was true. The more I researched the historical basis for the resurrection of Jesus, the more compelling the case became that he actually conquered the grave.[2] Yet, with all of that, I asked myself if I actually believed a dead person could conquer our worst enemy. I doubted simply because it is possible to do so, especially when the thing in question is so integral to one's worldview and so out of the ordinary. Though I was never intellectually confounded about such matters as the resurrection, I was occasionally baffled in my heart, in my soul.

Other times, however, my doubt has taken me in a different direction, appearing for instance as an emotional phenomenon, a personal uncertainty, or as the reaction to pain or hard circumstances.[3] These and other factors play a role in human doubt.

But, what is doubt? Is it lack of faith? At times this seems to be the case, for Jesus clearly rebuffs his disciples when they question his power and compassion. There is a kind of doubt that is lamentable, for it is associated with a mutinous attitude that blocks one's path to God. James captures this, instructing us that when a person requests something from God,

> he must ask in faith without any doubting, for the one who doubts is like the surf of the sea, driven and tossed by the wind. For that man ought not to expect that he will receive anything from the Lord, being a double-minded man, unstable in all his ways (1:6–8).

2. See Wright, *The Challenge of Easter.*
3. See DiCello, *Why?*

Instead of being wholeheartedly devoted to the Lord, here is an individual whose outlook is characterized by imbalance and insincerity.[4] This amounts to a lack of allegiance to God.[5]

Jesus struck a similar cord when, while traveling with his friends across a turbulent and threatening sea, he asked his frantic and self-absorbed disciples, "Why are you afraid? Do you still have no faith?" (Mark 4:40).

However, the fact that doubt can cause harm does not mean that it is always avoidable or that it is necessarily a bad thing. While it is common to label all doubt as harmful, Scripture clearly allows for a type of doubt that is proper and spiritually valuable.[6] Though some doubt is practically equivalent to unbelief, there is a type of uncertainty that can actually prompt faith, providing opportunities to stretch ourselves by looking to the One who is faith's true aim. What's more, it is certainly better to acknowledge doubt and to honestly persevere through it than it is to pretend that our faith is impenetrable. A limping faith is better than self-deception, and a wavering trust is more authentic and meaningful than feigned belief. It is vital to our spiritual well-being, in other words, to understand that we have to be honest with ourselves and with God.

In dealing with doubt, it is helpful to simply accept it as a part of the human condition. The key to faith is not our psychological disposition, our ability to sustain an unwavering confidence. Rather, the key to faith is its object. What makes our faith is not our capacity to work ourselves into a mental state of belief but the fact we are seeking the One who has pledged himself to us. From this perspective, even doubt has a faith-inducing capacity.

4. See Davids, *The Epistle of James*, 75.
5. See Moo, *James*, 64.
6. See Nystrom, *James*, 61.

Here's the point: you don't have to tie together every loose end. Though intellectual pursuits are important, they are never enough. At some point, if you're going to believe, you simply have to be able to say, "I don't have everything figured out. Doubts sometimes seize upon my mind, and certain answers don't completely satisfy me. But, despite these things, as I look at the big picture, I still believe."

I vividly recall a time in my life when, for reasons that I still don't fully understand, I went through a period of deep turmoil regarding my faith. In retrospect I think I brought a lot of it on myself by being overly introspective and demanding too many answers. Whatever the cause, I truly struggled with these issues. It was during this time that I came upon a short but meaningful song, based on Psalm 23 and sung by Steve Green. It's called Rest, and the words are still important to me.

> Rest, the Lord is near.
> Refuse to fear.
> Enjoy his love.[7]

My life at that time was actually quite good, and there weren't any particularly trying circumstances on which I could pin the blame for my emotional condition. What's more, I was quite familiar with the arguments for faith, being able to provide a solid basis for the truth I believed, so I wasn't tripped up by the facts. Rather, my battle was internal and personal, and so any help that I was going to receive had to address me in that capacity. Hence, the brilliance of Green's simple song. I could *Rest*, according to Green, because the Lord himself was with me. *Refuse to fear* reminded me that I didn't have to manufacture faith so much as I needed to fall into the arms and enjoy the benefits of the Lord who promised to meet me where I was. I can't tell you

7. Steve Green, Joy To The World, *Rest* 1987 (Sparrow Records).

how many times I played that song, basking in the presence of the One who met me in my doubt. Through tears and uncertainty, I gained stability. Doubt, when brought into the presence of God, can do that; it can yield assurance and confidence.

Doubt, in other words, is not always a bad thing. Being honest with ourselves, others, and especially God can be a pathway to an invigorated faith.[8] To this end, we are invited to join the Psalmist, other faithful men and women, and even Jesus himself, in declaring that there are times when our vision is cloudy and darkness surrounds us. But, amid doubt, light can fill our souls, and faith can not only survive but flourish. Perhaps this prayer—spoken by a man in response to the compassionate invitation of Jesus—is apt for all of us, as well. "I do believe; help my unbelief" (Mark 9:23–24).

Or, as Green said:

> Rest, the Lord is near.
> Refuse to fear.
> Enjoy his love.

8. Rightly construed, doubt has a number of potential benefits. For instance it can be a sure sign of humility, an acknowledgment that we don't know everything. Indeed, those who admit ignorance are much more likely to discover answers to their questions. Likewise, the sheer acknowledgment of doubt and uncertainty can prompt us to the most relevant posture of all, one of utter reliance on the One we seek. We are told, after all, that the humble and contrite encounter God (Psalm 51:17; Isaiah 57:15).

10

Holy Crap

when bad leads to good

It was a Friday and a payday when I hurried home from work. My plan was to get changed quickly, cash my check, and then dash off to meet some friends. As I rushed around the house, I realized that I had misplaced my paycheck. I looked upstairs and downstairs but could not locate the check. I searched the car, but it was not there. I even looked in drawers I hadn't opened, but it was nowhere to be found. After a while, to be honest, I was getting a bit frazzled. Knowing that I had an appointment to keep was one thing; being unable to leave for that appointment was, well, frustrating.

So, here I was running back and forth, in and out of the house, baffled by my situation and just plain angry. Then, when it seemed that matters could not get worse, I did it. I mean I *really* did it. While taking the dog out to do her duty, I managed to place my foot squarely on the one thing that could drive me over the edge. That's right; I stepped in dog crap. To be honest, though, at that juncture in my adventure, I was considering a cruder label. What I had in mind was a four letter word that rhymes with *fit*. In fact that's what I was on the verge of having, *a fit!*

At that moment, all I could do was scramble into the kitchen, grab a bunch of paper towels, and begin to clean my defiled shoe. So, that's what I did. I scraped and scrubbed as fast as I was able. Then, as I turned to place the shoe back on my foot, something caught my eye. No, it couldn't be . . . but there it was. Right before my eyes, sitting on the counter was—you guessed it—my check! I would not have noticed the check had I not bent over to replace my shoe, and I wouldn't have been doing that if I hadn't removed it in an effort to clean it. And, of course, none of this would have been possible had I not first stepped in my dog's "number 2." All I could do was smile.

Okay, so what's the moral of the story? Well, the lesson here might be to avoid being stupid enough to misplace an important thing like a paycheck. Or, a case could be made for watching where you place your foot, or for always keeping an extra pair of sneakers nearby. But, perhaps something else should capture our attention, which is this: It is possible for good to come from that which we would otherwise label bad. One can find a paycheck through the unlikely experience of stepping in dog dirt.

At issue here is the age-old problem of suffering and evil. Why does a good God allow bad things to happen to his people? How can he remain both benevolent and in control yet permit the terrible things we see all around us every day?

In our efforts to grasp this subject, we mustn't treat it in a superficial manner. My illustration certainly does *not* answer all of the questions concerning human pain. After all, why the need for a doggie doo-doo detour (try saying that four times fast) in my pursuit of the paycheck? Couldn't I have located my check without the mess? Likewise, why does God allow heartache, misery, confusion, relationship problems, and all of the hassles of life? Can't he get what he wants some other way? The problem of evil remains, and a *completely* satisfying answer to life's most baffling events is difficult to come by.

However, partial explanations *do* exist, and there is something to learn from my exasperating experience. One of the clues is located in the fact that God is the master storyteller. The Christian Scriptures are teeming with stories about God, his people, and their relationship to the world they encounter. Often, these involve men and women whose hearts are stretched and strained by their challenging circumstances. Yet, God is able to bring beauty out of that which is revolting. The supreme example of this is the death of Jesus.

Jesus was the consummate model of integrity, the paradigm of good, the perfect standard of love, and yet he was mistreated, beaten, mocked, spit upon, and eventually killed. When one takes into account the dignity of Jesus, that he is God's unique Son, the crimes committed against him are all the more horrific. But, as we learn, God was up to something in the death of his Son. Because of Jesus' death, we receive life. Due to his cross work, our wrongs are blotted out, and we are admitted into the presence of God. In other words the worst of events becomes the avenue through which the greatest of outcomes is made possible. Amazingly, God can take what is despicable and turn it into a blessing.

Without minimizing the legitimate struggles that many good and honest people face, we can at least say that God often works *through* the things we consider troublesome or inconvenient to create that which contributes to our ultimate good. We can't always identify his ways or how his providence benefits us. But it is a comfort to realize that he knows what he's doing as he directs our steps, tells his story, and, puzzling as it may appear, brings right out of wrong, good out of evil, blessing out of the appalling features of life. Something to keep in mind the next time you step into life's equivalent of dog manure.

11

Something Stinks

gauging our spirituality

ALL OF US HAVE had the experience of sitting next to someone who, how shall I put it, someone who challenges our
olfactory membranes with his or her distinct and unpleas-
ant body odor. Sometimes, it is the result of a completed
bout of exercise. Vigorous activity produces perspiration,
which carries a distinct aroma. Most of the time, we read-
ily endure such odors, for they are temporary and easily
remedied by means of a quick shower. On the other hand,
there are also those unfortunate individuals who, quite
frankly, lack personal hygiene and who therefore give off
an offensive scent. While we should feel compassion for
such people, and though we can try to assist them, it surely
cannot be denied that they, well, they smell.

What is interesting about this subject is the fact that
these unsanitary individuals don't usually mind spreading

their odors. Perhaps, they just don't care what others think; thus, the aroma they spread is as trivial to them as the color of the shoes they are wearing. Most of the time, however, I suspect that they are so used to their own scent that they don't really notice it. In either case there are numerous people who suffer (or make others suffer) from a lack of cleanliness.

Well, the other day I had an encounter with such a person, and a new thought dawned on me. I wondered, "What if I smell too?" After all, I had sprinkled cologne on myself earlier that day, and I wasn't able to detect its fragrance. Similarly, maybe I wouldn't even notice it if I were to permeate the air with a pungent aura.

Now, all of this discussion about bad smells set me to thinking about another type of odor, a spiritual one. Are there times, I contemplated, when some foul stench of mine causes others to gag? Might there be some repugnancy to me about which I'm not even aware? Perhaps, this explains the reactions of some who find it difficult remaining in my vicinity for very long. Maybe, I just plain stink!

From these thoughts on aroma, we find a metaphor for the way we live our lives before God. Among other things, we can say the following:

Sometimes, our lives are disconnected from God, and we don't even know it. It's amazing, is it not, how oblivious we can be to our own inabilities, weaknesses, and shameful behavior. What we take as an ordinary human quality can be a mark of self-deception. It is possible, in other words, to get so used to our profane lifestyle that is seems quite normal. We can smell bad and not even know it! Scary thought, indeed.

It is possible to live half-heartedly. There is in Scripture a reference to "a double minded" person, someone who is spiritually unstable. This is the person who, though not necessarily troubled about his imperfections, is aware that others might be. As a result, he leads a kind of double existence, appearing to care about various positive matters but doing so half heartedly.

This reminds me of those times when I used to carry talcum powder with me to the gym. Thus, if I were in a hurry, I'd workout and then sprinkle myself with talcum powder to cover the odor. I would half-jokingly refer to this as an artificial shower. The point is that while I knew that I needed to wash up, I was temporarily satisfied with a little talcum powder.[1] The smell of perspiration remained, but I tried to mask it. So, it can be with our lives. We can put on a show for others, enough to make them believe we are doing well, while all the while hiding our true condition.

Our spiritual health can depend on the intervention of others. Let's be honest. We weren't meant to go at it alone. We need others, which is what spiritual friendship is all about. This means that there will be times when we must intervene in another's life, showing that person a better way. To return to our metaphor, there are times when we must point people to the shower. To paraphrase Galatians 6:1, "Gently instruct those who smell to 'come clean.' But don't be proud, for you too tend to pick up some rather repulsive odors."

Only Jesus can ultimately remove the odors of life. This is the essence of the good news. Jesus came to earth to rescue those deserving of condemnation. We were doing our thing, smelling quite unclean. We deserved rejection and a one way trip to the garbage dump. But God had another plan, for Jesus went to the place of refuse in our place so that we, trusting in him, might avoid such a destiny. Of course God isn't finished with us yet. Though he has provided a right standing before God through the rescuing activity of his Son, and while he has redirected our lives, we still have a tendency to pick up a certain odor now and

1. The reference here, of course, is to the powder that is used to freshen up. See, for example, http://www.johnsonsbaby.com.

then. Thank God—and I say it reverently—he has provided the spiritual soap that cleanses us from our many wrongs.[2]

So, what about you? Are you making bad choices and so exuding a type of spiritual stench? Do people know you are coming before you arrive? Most importantly, what does your Maker think of you? The solution to this dilemma is not to fear, run, and hide in one of the world's trash cans. Neither is it to get lost in an endless array of religious activities, the talcum powder of life. What you need, what we all need, is the One who alone can remove our odors. Those who bathe in his love can't help but get clean.

---

2. "If we confess our sins, He is faithful and righteous to forgive us our sins and to cleanse us from all unrighteousness" (1 John 1:9).

12

Where Are My Pants?

divine providence and
the way things often work out

THE DAY OF MY brother Mark's wedding was a time of tremendous jubilation. After years of searching for that "special someone," Mark had finally found Kristen. When the time was right, the wedding date was set, and everyone was excited. In fact it was my immense honor to be the Best Man in my brother's wedding. Thus, I got to plan the pre-wedding dinner at a nice local restaurant. It fell on me to give the toast on the big day. And, of course, I had the privilege of standing next to my brother during the actual wedding ceremony.

However, one slight problem almost brought my participation to an end. About two hours before the wedding I realized something quite unexpected; I had forgotten the pants to my tuxedo! That's right, as I began to change for the ceremony, which was to take place at a church about an hour from our hometown, I realized that I had somehow forgotten my wedding pants.

At that juncture, no one who was aware of this dilemma knew what to do. We were too far from home to make the trip to pick up the pants. My wife, who was coming down separately, was already well on her way. And there I was, the best man, lacking an integral piece of my wedding attire.

To be honest, we initially hid this information from Mark. He already had a lot on his plate, and we certainly didn't want to do anything to tarnish this day. So, we contemplated and wondered and schemed. Then it took place, the miracle we were waiting for. Jason, Mark's soon-to-be brother-in-law, just happened to have an extra pair of tuxedo pants with him, and they just happened to fit me . . . perfectly. How, you might ask, is this possible? After all, most people don't carry a spare pair of pants with them to a wedding.

Here's the short version: Mark's tuxedo supplier lives in our home town, while Mark's future brother-in-law, Jason, lived some distance away. On the day we were all going to be fitted, Jason wasn't available, and so he was not completely certain about the style or size he should wear. As a result, Mark decided to order two different styles, which Jason took with him to the church on Mark's wedding day.

If Jason had been available for his fitting, he would not have had a second pair of pants, and I would have been out of luck on the big day. If he had not decided to bring a second pair to the church with him, I would have been in trouble. If the pants themselves were the wrong size, I would have been, at the least, wearing over or undersized pants for the duration of the wedding and reception. If any one of a series of events or decisions had taken place, I would have been lacking one essential aspect of my wedding garb, my pants! Yet, somehow, everything fell into place, and I was able to participate in my brother's wedding without a hitch.

In retrospect, of course, the whole situation is comical, and we all laughed as we finally told Mark what had taken place without his knowledge. How in the world could I neglect to take my pants with me to my brother's wedding? It was like a scene from some sitcom. But, besides the humorous side of this incident, there are also lessons here about life.

When things are not going according to plan, we tend to panic. This is especially the case when the circumstances in which we find ourselves are truly outside of our control. I was without pants in a place where an extra pair are not normally available. Yet, amazingly, an extra pair appeared. So it is with life.

How many times have you found yourself in a situation in which you thought there was no way out? Ever been stressed out about things outside your power, by a situation that seemed headed in a bad direction? Yet, how often, in these same circumstances, has everything worked out, and how frequently have you discovered that what you thought was catastrophic was actually something much less, perhaps even something amusing?

It is important, of course, not to minimize those circumstances of life that are indeed dire and life-altering. Sometimes when what we encounter seems bad, it truly is bad. Thus, not everything we come up against is to be quickly classified as simple.

Still, it is surely the case that many of the things we get upset about are not as awful as we initially thought. While we might feel like the world is coming to an end or that some major problem is imminent, this is not usually the case. Though we do not want to make light of those events that seem genuinely serious, we also must avoid making things much worse than they actually are.

The secret, I think, is being able to relax enough to see the big picture and to recognize that life is not as out of control as we sometimes imagine it to be. From God's perspective, in fact, life is never out of control, for it is always governed by a good and wise Creator. The bottom line is that God is bigger and better than we give him credit for.

So, you find yourself in circumstances that are the equivalent of being at a wedding with no pants. Hang on, trust in God, and know that somehow he will work everything out. Indeed, as you're waiting for him to "show up," recognize that he is already there with you. You are loved by a compassionate, strong, and faithful God (with a sense of humor), and nothing is outside of his influence, not even a pair of pants! Perhaps that will be enough to make you believe . . . and smile!

13

Why Can't We See Jesus?

finding God in one another

Some years ago, my mother-in-law passed away, which prompted a series of rather deep questions from my then nine-year-old and four-year-old sons. You see, this was their first close-encounter with death.

One of the earlier questions was, "Where is Nana?" to which I responded, "We believe she is in heaven." But a day or so later, they posed this question: "Why can't we see Jesus?" We talk about him all of the time. So, where is he?

I smiled at the simple profundity of my children. At first, I offered a standard answer: "Jesus became a man and lived among us for a short time. After he was crucified, God raised him from the grave. Then, he returned to be with his Father until the time when he returns to the earth. We can't see him because he is in heaven."

Upon reflection, however, I have wondered if perhaps my sons' question should be taken even more seriously.

During my morning jog, I pondered what it meant to "see" God. In one sense it makes sense that we can't see him. Not only is Jesus (the visible manifestation of God) with the Father, but God in his essence is a spirit being, after all, which means that he is invisible to our natural senses.

Yet, God can surely be seen in many ways. In nature, his imprint is evident. Through his Word, he communicates and moves us to follow him. And one of the chief ways he has chosen to disclose himself is by means of his people. While he is never limited by our imperfections, it is true that, amazing as it sounds, he wants to make himself known through us.

A number of biblical texts come to mind. "Let your light shine before men in such a way that they will see your good works and glorify your Father who is in heaven" (Matthew 5:16). "If we love one another, God abides in us" (1 John 4:11). "We are ambassadors for Christ, as though God were entreating through us" (2 Corinthians 5:20).

This means that God wants to use us in such a way that we genuinely communicate his presence to those we meet. In a very real sense, we are to be living conduits of his mercy and love, channels of his grace, and one of the avenues by which he manifests himself.

My mother-in-law certainly gave expression to these qualities, as do my wife and my budding theologian children. At times, though, I am not so sure about myself. How inconsistent many of us can be, and how unlike the Savior, whose sacred life we are supposed to mirror.

One day, of course, Jesus will pierce the sky. One day we will see God in an unmistakable manner. One day, faith will give way to sight. But until then, I hope that, despite our many inadequacies, we become better "transmitters" of the living Lord. Though Jesus has yet to return to planet earth, he really shouldn't be hidden from our sight. Maybe, it would do us all some good to honestly consider my boys' question. In your life and mine, why can't more people see Jesus?

PART 3

Faith's Perspective

Certain key ideas provide the context for believing.
A variety of truths impact the attitude of believers
and so bolster faith.

14

Vapors of Hope

realistic optimism

> "Whoever dies with the most toys wins."
> "Life's a bitch, and then you die."
> "Don't take life too seriously; you won't get out alive."

THESE AND SIMILAR SENTIMENTS express the somber but accurate assessment that there are some things in life that we cannot escape. Try as we might, we cannot avoid all pain. Pretend as we may, we cannot escape the grave. Wish as we please, we simply cannot get away from some rather harsh realities that threaten to suck the life out of life.

Of course this idea is nothing new. The author of Ecclesiastes, many centuries ago, said: "Vanity of vanities! All is vanity" (Ecclesiastes 1:2). The term *vanity* means a vapor, something that is difficult or impossible to grasp. As Ecclesiastes puts it, even the most noble of tasks is "chasing after the wind" (Ecclesiastes 1:14).

Part 3: Faith's Perspective

There is something about life, when faced honestly, which utterly rattles us. Life is temporary, fleeting, and out of our control. Each day is an unstable thing, which explains why so many of us do whatever we can to bury, run from, or escape such depressing notions. One wonders how many of our legitimate daily affairs are in some ways efforts to crowd out thoughts of life's frailty and temporariness.

We spend much time in our society trying to prolong life but, however successful our attempts, we all eventually die. Many put forth great energy in seeking to accumulate things—gadgets and toys that are intended to amuse, or else to show off. But whatever the efforts, the toys will eventually deteriorate and even what survives will be inherited by someone else.

Some, with perhaps more noble motives, want to create a legacy for themselves, passing on whatever they can by way of material wealth and inheritance, but this, too, will be lost to time. Certain individuals want to be memorialized by building a reputation that survives the grave. This way, it is thought, even after they are gone, others will appreciate the achievements and remember the names of their predecessors. But how many people leave this kind of mark? We're familiar with an Abraham Lincoln, an Albert Einstein, or a Babe Ruth, but few of us are consistently captivated by what even these admittedly remarkable individuals, now long gone, have done. What's more, these famous figures are not here to enjoy their own accomplishments or personally benefit from their acts of nobility, intellect, and athleticism. And, let's face it, even those of us who truly appreciate the achievements of our predecessors can only do so for a limited time, for we too will one day pass from the scene.

Perhaps another will say, "My hope is to pass on traits and ideals that my children and grandchildren will enjoy for years to come." Yet, even here, there is no guarantee that anyone's children and grandchildren will take heed to what their parents and grandparents worked so hard to promote and embody. And, again, even if we successfully pass on high ideals to our descendents, they too will be swallowed by the grave.

These admittedly gloomy thoughts are hard to manage, which is precisely why so many people spend a lifetime running from them. Yet, depressing as it might be, the assessment is accurate. So, we must ask, *is* life truly meaningless? Is there nothing to be gained from all that we say and do during our sojourn on earth? Is it all a waste?

Contrary to what one might initially think, the author of Ecclesiastes does not want us to abandon hope. Indeed, in a number of places, he states what we all intuitively know, that life *does* have meaning As Ecclesiastes notes, God has "made everything appropriate in its time. He has also set eternity in their hearts" (3:11). Here, we find a key to understanding how life, though sometimes appearing to be pointless, is actually filled with meaning. Ultimate purpose is linked to a relationship with our transcendent-immanent Maker.

If we consider life "under the sun" as an end in itself, if we treat life as if it is unrelated to God, then everything takes on a depressing hue. If no one remembers, if all that we work hard for is eventually taken from us, if even our best intentions are squandered and lost, our lives are futile. As another writer records: "If the dead are not raised, Let us eat and drink, for tomorrow we die" (1 Corinthians 15:32). In other words, if what we observe around us is all that there is, we might as well drown out our inconsequential existence.

But, and this is the point of Ecclesiastes, there *is* something more, and that something is located in the One who created us for himself. And the point here is not merely that doing right today will yield benefits in eternity, as true as that is, but that life "under the sun" takes on meaning precisely because it is life that flows from and to God.

This is why, for instance, we read that "there is nothing better for them than to rejoice and to do good in one's lifetime; moreover, that every man who eats and drinks sees good in all his labor—it is the gift of God" (Ecclesiastes 3:12). Joy and goodness are meaningful because they come from God.

Is life sad and filled with uncertainty and frustration? Yes, it is, and we would do well to recognize this and lead our lives in ways that reflect reality. But there is also much more here, for these dispiriting thoughts are intended to turn us outside of ourselves. Life is futile only when separated from the Divine. Life does have meaning when lived from the vantage point of our Creator.

Our efforts to achieve goals in this life are completely proper because they stem from a meaning-making God, and so they have enduring relevance. While our goods will eventually deteriorate, our noble attempts to accumulate and share them will not be forgotten by the Lord of heaven and earth. Though death comes for all of us, we also have an instinctive awareness that this life is a passageway to an even fuller existence. That future life is impacted by the choices we make in the here-and-now.

Our responsibility is to recognize the futility of life outside of God and to embrace him as the One through whom "every good and perfect gift" comes (James 1:17). Despite the hard-to-handle features of life—its brevity and uncertainty and pain—there is joy and purpose when we see and live this life through the template God has provided.

As the book of Ecclesiastes draws to a close, we receive these instructions:

> The conclusion, when all has been heard, is: fear
> God and keep His commandments, because this

applies to every person. For God will bring every act to judgment, everything which is hidden,
whether it is good or evil (12:13–14).

Life is a vapor, impossible to completely manage and often vexing. These facts humble us and can tend to drive us to despair. But hope remains as we turn our hearts to God, believing that the things of this life, even the harsh and difficult things, do indeed reflect and serve an ultimate purpose.

Here, then, is the lesson: We are meant to look to God, seeing our lives as joined to him who is both above us and with us, honoring him and embracing a life of godly integrity; these are the things that will last throughout this life and into the next. As the Contemporary English Version puts it: "Everything you were taught can be put into a few words: "Respect and obey God! This is what life is all about" (Ecclesiastes 12:13–14). With a humble, buoyant faith and a respectful allegiance to God, there is reason to retain optimism, for even the vapors of this life contain the seeds of eternal hope.

15

God Sees the Dust

doing right when no one is looking

A NUMBER OF YEARS ago, I assisted a friend who had a cleaning business. On certain days, we helped sweep, clean, vacuum, and otherwise beautify an office. I recall that on certain occasions, if I happened to be in a particularly meticulous mood, I would try to do an exceptionally thorough job. One night, I remember dusting the top of a soda machine. The dust there was pretty thick, which is understandable given that it was in such an out-of-the-way place.

To accomplish my chore, I had to stand on top of a chair, remove a number of objects from the top of the machine, and then clean areas that few if any would ever see. This is what got me thinking. Here I was doing extra work, not only the typical chores but those things that no one would likely notice. Even if someone had surveyed the top of the soda machine, he would not know how dirty it had been previously, nor would anyone realize how superb a dusting job I had done. Indeed, I had wiped away the evidence!

Have you ever wondered about the purpose of doing things that no one sees? Ever done the right thing only to be ignored for it? Have you ever asked yourself if there is no real benefit to doing right when no one is looking? Among our greatest incentives is that God does indeed see all things, and one day there will be a reward. Though I cannot completely envision it, God will bless us in his good time. It may be in this life or perhaps in the next. Either way, God is paying attention.

So, you're really trying to do a good job, going above typical expectations, and yet you're cognizant that most people aren't paying attention. You're dusting the top of a soda machine that no one even cares about. Jesus has these words to say:

> Take care! Don't do your good deeds publicly, to be admired, because then you will lose the reward from your Father in heaven. When you give a gift to someone in need, don't shout about it as the hypocrites do—blowing trumpets in the synagogues and streets to call attention to their acts of charity! I assure you, they have received all the reward they will ever get. But when you give to someone, don't tell your left hand what your right hand is doing. Give your gifts in secret, and your Father, who knows all secrets, will reward you. (Matthew 6:1–4, NLT)

Yeah, there will be times when your good works are overlooked, your best efforts ignored or downplayed, and your contributions not even noticed. When during these times you are tempted to give up, when discontentment seizes you, just remember that the ever-present Lord knows what's going on even if no one else does. Trust him, for he sees even the dust.

16

Ears to Hear

listen to the music

His heart just wasn't in it. Though Rocky was supposed to be preparing for a huge boxing match, he couldn't find the motivation and the courage to prepare for his opponent. To make matters worse, Adrian, his wife, who has opposed this fight from the beginning, now lay comatose in a hospital bed. Rocky, for his part, is dejected and lacking any direction, hoping and praying that Adrian will awake from her slumber.

Adrian does finally revive, and when she does, she calls Rocky to her side, whispering her request: "I want you to do one thing," she says. Then, a moment later, she completes her thought, uttering the word that propels Rocky to new heights. "Win!" Adrian's wish for her husband is that he would win.

At this point in the movie, Mickey, Rocky's trainer, famously asks, "What are we waiting for?" And from that moment forward, we encounter a rejuvenated Rocky, a hard-working and energized fighter, with the scene portrayed in such a way that many of us want to live vicariously through him. Indeed, I recall one late evening, some time ago, when, after seeing Rocky III, a friend of mine and I went out for a three mile jog in about a foot of freshly fallen snow! Rocky does that for you, or at least for me.

But, what is it that highlights the touching moments of a movie? What draws out the emotion in us? What makes us want to embody the best features of the films we watch? Perhaps, more than anything else it's the music.

Immediately after Adrian gives her approval to Rocky, following right on the heels of Mickey's "What are we waiting for?" the music begins, building to a crescendo, carrying us with it, highlighting the heart stirring features of the moment. It's the music that turns a nice story into a truly inspiring tale, and it's like this in almost every film. What would Jaws be like without the Dun Dun? Sure, we'd have a large shark, lurking in the waters nearby, but it wouldn't be the same without the music. The same holds true for such notable films as Titanic, Forest Gump, Chariots of Fire, Casablanca, and a host of movies and television shows. The music is like an emotional magnifying glass, drawing to the surface the truth and significance of any important scene.

Of course some would argue that this is what makes movies magical or make-believe. The director gets to dub in music at the appropriate time. As I once read on a t-shirt: "The problem with life is that it lacks the background music." Real life, or so we are told, differs from a movie. In the real world, there are no emotion-laden soundtracks . . . or are there? Though some concur with the sentiment of the above-mentioned t-shirt, others assert that the t-shirt is mistaken. Perhaps the music *is* playing!

Indeed, a type of music is playing all around us each day. That's why, at least on occasion, certain moments in our lives are filled with greater significance and unusual zeal. Sometimes, the things we encounter and the people to whom we relate bring out deep feelings and powerful emotions. Though we may go lengthy periods of time in a rather perfunctory fashion, every so often ardor fills our souls, we move beyond the superficial, and we become much more sensitive to the profundity of the life God has granted us. At such times empathy flows, and we see things the way they truly are. In other words we "hear the music."

All too often, unfortunately, it takes a trial or an experience of desperation for us to "hear the music," that is, to recognize what truly matters. But even beyond these wake-up call moments, most of us have at least occasionally grasped the extraordinary importance of people, relationships, opportunities, truth, and love. When these things occur, we are hearing the music.

On this view it's not so much that life copies movies as it is that good movies mirror the better aspects of life. The music is playing every day, and when we hear it, it is difficult to remain unaffected. People truly matter. Relationships matter. Truth matters. Love matters. A lot of things are important, but as fallen and imperfect creatures in a fallen and imperfect world we often fail to see (or, to hear) what is all around us. Sometimes, the music is crowded out by the sheer craziness of our schedules or by the foolishness of our choices. But, and this is what we must remember, the music *is* playing, and my contention here is that the music Maker is the Lord of all things.

Our responsibility and privilege is to tune our ears to the sounds that are playing all around us. We do this best, when our souls are filled with good news, our minds deeply appreciative of the blessings we have received, our lives captivated by the possibilities that come to us each day, and our hearts keenly aware that the world is an amphitheater on which the Lord is playing his songs.

The music is playing. Hear the music.

17

The Simple Things

pondering everyday gifts

AT THE END OF the day, there is something extremely relevant and transformative about the simple things. Simple things—these are the things that enable us to feel a sense of belonging and purpose and comfort in our lives.

A short time ago, I was reminded of these simple things. After work, I was walking home, just basking in the beauty of the day. The sun was shining, the temperature was pleasant, and I was struck by the scene of two women who were hanging laundry on their respective clothes lines, simply chatting about who knows what. We exchanged hellos as I continued on my way. Then, a little while later, I saw my oldest son standing outside of our home, and he gave me a little wave when he saw me approaching from about a half block away—simple but for me carrying much meaning. A short time later, my youngest son also arrived at home with a friend, and being that they are runners, they quickly got changed before venturing outside for a jog around town. For my part, I simply relaxed, sipping on a nice cup of coffee and playing a little with the dogs. Again, it's the simple things.

I love the feeling of sitting around the house at night, when my wife and kids are all here with me.

I love the smell of freshly cut grass or of recently fallen rain.

I love to watch whatever television shows strike a nostalgic note within me, reminding me of the best of days-gone-by, and providing me with hope for similar future blessings.

I love the innocence of little (and not so little) children.

I love the camaraderie of family and friends.

I love the familiarity of following my favorite sports teams.

I love going for a jog over a local mountain on a brisk Saturday morning.

I love the regular routine of going to work, interacting with students (since I'm a teacher), and all that a typical day entails.

I love the simplicity of a warm cup of coffee.

Though I also love a measure of the spectacular, reveling in such things as riding roller coasters or taking long-awaited vacations, it's the simple things that truly make me tick. Thus, while I enjoy (and sometimes require) the weekend as much as anyone, I mostly look forward to the week. Though as a teacher I have the benefit of being away from the school for the summer, I honestly get excited about the fall and the beginning of the new school year. You see, it's the normal and the regular and the routine that shape us more than anything.

If you are blessed enough to experience any of these simple things, you are blessed indeed. And one of the reasons for this, I think, is that many of the simple things are given to us freely. They are gifts, in other words, undeserved and gracious bestowals of love from the great gift-Giver. As James put it: "every desirable and beneficial gift comes out of heaven" (1:17). Or, as the author of Ecclesiastes wrote: "And people should eat and drink and enjoy the fruits of their labor, for these are gifts from God" (3:12–13, NLT). That's it: the simple things are gifts. With a grateful heart, enjoy the gift of the simple things.

18

A Good Story

meeting God in his story and ours

I DON'T KNOW ABOUT your family, but when ours gets together it is fairly common for us to discuss our shared history. Sometimes, we retell relatively minor tales like the time we kids sneaked downstairs very early one Christmas morning to get a look at the latest additions to our toy collections. Our recollections of such occurrences bring smiles to our faces and a connection to days gone by. Of course some stories we recount are of a much more serious nature, such as the events surrounding the death of my uncle Ray some forty years ago. Uncle Ray was a history teacher and football coach, whose zeal for life was contagious. Though I was fairly young when he passed away, I still feel the impact of his life.

But why do we tell such stories? What makes them so important to us? While there are a number of reasonable explanations, I think the most basic one is that these stories somehow provide a sense of identity. When we tell them, we are in effect saying, "This is who we are. We are a people united by our common past." Somehow, the stories we tell draw us together, providing the impetus for the life we desire to live in the present and into the future.

Have you ever considered the fact that God loves stories? Indeed, he is the consummate storyteller. Think for a moment how much of the Bible is given to the communication of his stories. Among many others, we are told of the creation (Genesis 1:1–31), the great flood of Noah's day (Genesis 7:1–24), Daniel in the Lion's den (Daniel 6:4–27), and Moses and the Ėxodus from Egyptian tyranny (Exodus 12:33ff). Of course the greatest of them all is the story of Jesus. His birth, life, teachings, betrayal, death, and resurrection have been the topic of countless books, movies, lectures, discussions, and sermons. Again, God loves stories.

With all of these stories in Scripture, it is rather strange to find many ignoring this important element of the faith. Far too often, the church has specialized in formulaic faith. Study and repeat the right formula, recount the correct propositions, and somehow you'll do just fine spiritually. Though it would be foolish to ignore the propositional aspects of the faith, it is equally unwise to attempt to live our lives in a merely propositional fashion. It is not enough to simply store away facts. We must also connect with God himself through the stories he has left for our benefit.

One of the most invigorating, motivating, unity-promoting things we can do is to tell our stories. The narrative portions of Scripture draw us together in a common bond as we recount the history of our predecessors, as we repeat the accounts of God's intervention in the lives of people like us.

The stories of Scripture have many purposes. Sometimes, they warn us. Other times, they encourage. Very often, they cause us to marvel at the majestic ways of our Lord. Always, they remind us that the God who did such marvelous things in the past is also our God. Of course interpretive discernment teaches us to be careful not to misapply the narrative sections of Scripture. Still, the overall effect of the Bible's stories is to show us that the Lord is an active, involved, intervening deity, and he cares for his people.

Often, when our family shares its stories, I leave our gatherings feeling refreshed and much closer to the other members of the family. Our family narrative somehow works its way into our hearts and draws us together. In a similar yet even more profound way, the narrative aspects of Scripture are intended to work their "magic." Noah, Abraham, and Moses are entry points into a relationship with the God who not only invaded their lives but enters ours as well. Matthew, Mark, Luke, and John are snapshots of the divine-human Savior in action. As we trace his steps, examining his story, we find ourselves somehow connecting with him.

It is unfortunate that in certain circles the stories of the Bible are treated like a mere addendum to faith, curios and interesting, but not all that relevant. A more balanced reading of Scripture reveals that these stories play a critical role in both our spiritual development and our efforts to encourage others. Certainly, we must give due weight to the essential ideas that are associated with faith; Scripture contains propositional truths and explanations of historical occurrences. But, as important as these are, we must not neglect the stories God has revealed.

Jesus loved to tell stories because they disclosed God in a way that nothing else could. We, too, can enter the greatest story ever told, the story he is still telling in the lives of those who listen for his voice. His grace allows us to be a part of the narrative, the ongoing drama of our journey with God.

There's nothing like a good story. What's yours?

19

Pi . . . and God

*3.14159265358979323846264338327950288
4197169399375105 . . .*

THIS IS PI, YOU know, the number used to express the ratio of a circumference of a circle to its diameter. I first became fascinated with Pi when, as a little kid, I heard that it was a number with no end. Pi, I learned those many years ago, is a never-ending number. Computers have calculated Pi to trillions of digits, and this doesn't even begin to scratch the surface of Pi, for Pi never ends.

It was probably the idea of the infinite that first boggled my mind when I was young, and now, years later, I think the whole notion of infinity somehow reminds me of other immeasurable things. Here is a number that is endless; it sounds almost spiritual, for a number of God-related matters are also without end.[1]

1. Indeed, Carl Sagan's novel *Contact* suggests that the Creator may have hidden a message within the digits of Pi. See Sagan, *Contact.*

Think of it. According to Scripture, God's existence is without beginning or end. We measure things in years, decades, centuries, millennia, and ages, but these pale in comparison with the infinite. No matter how far back in time you could travel, you would never reach a point where God wasn't already there. If you were to travel into the future, God's end would never be in sight; indeed, there is no end, as there is no beginning.

Try to imagine how this applies to the future state of believers. However we define eternity (in years or as something completely different), the truth is that it never ends. This life is filled with uncertainty and sadness, and eventually comes to an end. But that life, like Pi, has no such limitations. What must it be like to live life—an unimaginably full life, at that—without thought of interruption? Not only are the graves emptied, but the cemeteries are no longer required. In the grace and wisdom of God, we will be alive forevermore. What a thought!

What's more, we can easily apply this concept of the unlimited to God's traits. If he is powerful, he is *all* powerful (omnipotence). If he possesses knowledge, he has *all* knowledge (omniscience). If he is present, he is *everywhere* present (omnipresence). As Pi is infinite, defying our ability to measure, so the Lord of all things is incalculably great. He is the beginning and the end because he has no beginning and will have no end.

The most incredible thing of all, however, is that this infinite being, the living God, took on finiteness. God became a man. More so, he became a human being in order to experience the ignominious death of the cross. A greater contrast could not be envisioned. The Alpha and Omega became a human being in order to rescue human beings.

This mind-boggling condescension shows the length God will go to in order to secure our standing before him, in order to establish our link with him. "He who was rich became poor" says Scripture (2 Corinthians 8:9). This is love beyond compare, love that motivated our spiritual rescue, love that inspires authentic living.

3.14159265358979323846264338327950502 ... God gave us a number without end, a number we can explore but not exhaust, a number we can express but only in small measure. Hmm, sounds a bit like God. We scratch the surface of his goodness and endeavor to comprehend his grace. Eternity will be for exploring the infinities of our Maker and Savior, the incomprehensible and boundless love of God.

20

Aunt Louise and *Ex Nihilo*
brief thoughts on cake and the creator

WHEN I WAS A kid, I used to help my Aunt Louise make cakes from scratch. She did most of the work, of course, but I assisted. Together we collaborated on these baking projects, creating many a tasty dessert.

It's pretty cool that we can create. Indeed, human beings are extremely gifted, being able to invent all kinds of gadgets and gizmos and countless useful (and useless) creations. We have this capacity, of course, because we are made in the image of the master Creator. He creates, and so we, like him, are able to make things.

But here's the crazy thing: When we create, we make use of materials that already exist. God, on the other hand, doesn't need to use a thing. My aunt was good, but I'm pretty sure she would have had trouble creating a cake without flour, butter, sugar, and various other ingredients.

Part 3: Faith's Perspective

There's an old Latin phrase, *ex nihilo*, which means "out of nothing." In the beginning God created *out of nothing*. Let this filter through your mind for a little while. God stood at the edge of nothingness and created everything. With no raw materials with which to work, the Maker began to make the cosmos. With no spare parts to utilize, God spoke the universe into existence.

Like I've said, we have the capacity to make some pretty amazing stuff. But we cannot make bikes, cars, buildings, sports stadiums, works of art, etc., *out of nothing*. Much less do we possess the ability to create atoms, quarks, strong and weak nuclear forces, light, galaxies, planets, or anything else you can think of . . . *out of nothing*!

So, what's the point? I guess it's that this God people talk about (or curse), this being to whom we owe our very existence, far exceeds our ability to completely grasp. Consider this the next time you gather your tools and your parts or your baking materials to create whatever it is you are planning to make. God created *out of nothing. Ex nihilo*—the very thought is astonishing.[1]

1. Assuming, as Big Bang cosmology indicates, that the universe had a beginning, God was the cause of this beginning. Given that there was nothing to begin with (i.e., no components or parts), his original creation was necessarily out-of-nothing. However, this does not limit God's ability to also create out of the things he originally made. Thus, God's creative capacity entails both the ex nihilo variety and the use-of-existing-building-blocks type.

21

God's Talk

detecting the transcendent

FOR AS LONG AS I can remember, I've been fascinated with the stars. Even as a young boy, I would stare up at the night sky and marvel. As a result, I've always been a science-fiction buff and a lover of various alien-oriented television shows and movies. When I was very young, in fact, I was so captivated by the heavens that I longed to be an astronaut. Though time and other interests would push me in a different direction, I've never lost my enthrallment with space.

Now, the reasons for my fascination with stars are probably numerous, but one seems always to stand above the others. When I gaze at the seemingly countless specs of light in the sky, I sense something bigger, something magnificent, something transcendent.

Of course many pundits would argue that this sense of a greater purpose is an illusion. According to them, we are merely a chance happening in an ultimately meaningless universe. Though I have considered this and similar views, I have to admit that I cannot get away from this inner cognizance that we are indeed a part of something greater, and I am not alone.

In countless ways, it seems, we participate in something that is grand and difficult to completely fathom. This is why the great majority of people down through history—from simple folks to scholars—have agreed with this assessment. While the details may vary, most of us have an inherent awareness of something that is indeed greater than we are. In fact it's not simply the stars that prompt this response. The fragrance of a flower, the birth of a child, the magnificence of a sunrise, the utter beauty of an authentic and devoted relationship, the rightness of love and compassion, the inherent desire for justice and fairness, the quest for truth, the unrelenting hope that springs from the human soul—these and countless other illustrations provide more than a hint of the transcendent.

What this means, of course, is that one key characteristic of human beings is that we gravitate to that which is larger than ourselves. That is, we have a certain affinity for those matters that are bigger and more relevant than any of us, greater than all of us. The Hebrew Bible describes an idea that corresponds with this, *the imago dei* (i.e., the image of God). There is a connection between the world around us and ourselves. Thus, we possess an inborn link of sorts to the speaking God, the God who reveals himself in and through his creation. As the Psalmist states: "The heavens are telling of the glory of God; And their expanse is declaring the work of His hands" (Psalm 19:1). One might say that God is manifesting himself in a myriad of ways each and every day. Something to keep in mind the next time you ponder the starry expanse.

Conclusion

STORIES—WE ALL HAVE THEM, and sometimes they illustrate greater spiritual realities. Those I've shared here portray some extremely significant truths. Among other things, we've seen that faith must be correctly understood and sincerely embraced. We've been reminded that we can thrive even when surrounded by those features of life that are puzzling and painful. Furthermore, we've considered that God is able to sustain, strengthen, and motivate those who contemplate his works and ways.

The truly amazing thing, of course, is that this God is actually with us, and he cares. Thus, the reason we can identify such vital and noble themes is because we live within the sphere of his influence. The transcendent-immanent God loves you and me, and he invites us to commune with him each day. Consider just a sampling of his compassionate requests:

"Turn to Me and be saved, all the ends of the earth; For I am God, and there is no other."[1]

"Call to Me and I will answer you, and I will tell you great and mighty things, which you do not know."[2]

1. Isaiah 45:22.
2. Jeremiah 3:33.

"You will seek Me and find Me when you search for Me with all your heart"[3]

"Come to Me, all who are weary and heavy-laden, and I will give you rest."[4]

Though God is in many ways mysterious, he makes himself known in and through our lives. The Maker and Sustainer of all things is a talking God, and in his great mercy and grace he woos us to himself. What about you? Do you sense his imprint in your life? Are you able to recognize the echoes of his love and truth? Amid the distractions of daily living, can you hear his call? His words are simple yet profound: "Follow Me."[5]

---

3. Jeremiah 29:13.
4. Matthew 11:28.
5. Mark 1:17, 8:34; John 8:12, 10:27.

Bibliography

David, Peter H. *The Epistle of James*. NIGTC. Grand Rapids, MI: William B. Eerdmans, 1982.

DiCello, Carmen C. *Truth in Balance: Doing Apologetics in a Postmodern Culture*. Eugene, OR: Wipf & Stock, 2009.

———. *Why? Reflections on the Problem of Evil*. Eugene, OR: Wipf & Stock, 2007.

Dodd, Patton. *My Faith So Far: A Story of Conversion and Confusion*. San Francisco, CA: Jossey-Bass, 2005.

Green, Steve. Joy To The World, *Rest* 1987 (Sparrow Records).

Main, Bruce. *Spotting the Sacred: Noticing God in the Most Unlikely Places*. Grand Rapids, MI: Baker, 2006.

Moo, Douglas J. *James*. Tyndale New Testament Commentaries. Grand Rapids, MI: InterVarsity, 1985.

Newbigin, Leslie. *Truth to Tell: The Gospel as Public Truth*. Grand Rapids, MI: William B. Eerdmans, 1991.

Nystrom, David P. *James*. The NIV Application Commentary. Grand Rapids, MI: Zondervan, 1997.

Sagan, Carl. *Contact*. New York, NY: Pocket, 1997.

Wright, N. T. *The Challenge of Easter*. Downers Grove, IL: InterVarsity, 2009.

———. *Simply Christian: Why Christianity Makes Sense*. New York, NY: Harper Collins, 2006.

Credits

Rest
Words and Music by Greg Nelson and Phill McHugh
Copyright © 1985 Greg Nelson Music, Universal Music—
Brentwood Benson Songs and River Oaks Music
All Rights for River Oaks Music Controlled and Adminis-
tered at EMICMGPublishing.com
All Rights Reserved Used by Permission
Reprinted by Permission of Hal Leonard Corporation

If you would like to contact Carmen DiCello, he can be reached at carmen1978@comcast.net.